W9-CJX-923

SMALL APPLIANCE REPAIR:
HEATER TYPES

THEODORE AUDEL & CO.

a division of

 HOWARD W. SAMS & CO., INC.
4300 West 62nd Street
Indianapolis, Indiana 46268

FIRST EDITION

FIRST PRINTING—1975

International Standard Book Number: 0-672-23801-2

Preface

The most important reason for you to repair your own small household appliances is probably the savings involved. Whether you do them for this reason or for the self-satisfaction of accomplishment, the information in this book will help you do an adequate repair job.

The majority of the troubles that affect heater-type home appliances—bad line cords, open heating elements, stuck switches and thermostats, etc.—can be fixed by the average homeowner with regular tools. If you know what the appliance is supposed to do and how it does it, you will have little trouble getting it to work again.

What this book does is tell you how these appliances work; shows you photographs and drawings of the inside parts and how they are assembled, and how to take them apart. Everyday language is used to explain how the basic parts work.

All heater-type appliances are basically a piece of resistance wire that gets hot when electric current is passed through it. If the heater does not get hot, we show you how to find out why, and how to fix it.

In addition, you will learn how to spot potential dangers before they can cause a fire or injure someone in the family by electrical shock. It is easy to do a proper repair job—no mathematical formulas, no special test instruments—just practical ways to make repairs safe and easy.

Robert Wel

Contents

Unit 1

Unit 2

Unit 3

Unit 4

Unit 5

Unit 6

SECTION

1

Introduction

Most of the troubles that cause heating-type home appliances to go bad can be fixed by the average homeowner with a few simple tools. If you know what an appliance is supposed to do, it is usually very simple to find out what is not working, and make the necessary repairs or adjustments to get it working again.

BASIC TOOLS

You will need as basic tools a couple of small screwdrivers; a pair of long-nosed pliers; and two simple test lamps that can be made easily from some sockets taken from a set of old Christmas tree lights, some wire, and 1 replacement-type electrical plug. A candy thermometer may also be added to the above list to use in testing for the proper adjustment of the heat controls on the appliance under repair.

The tools needed are shown in Fig. 1. The construction of the two test lamps is shown in detail in Fig. 2. The light socket is cut from the string of Christmas tree lights and attached to two probes made of heavy insulated solid wire. A sleeve of cardboard made from the tubes from a clothes hanger of the type that has the bottom part made of cardboard tubing, is slipped over the heavy wire and the connections are then taped securely with electrical tape. This method makes a safe sure test lamp. One of the lamps is used for continuity tests, which will be explained later. The other is used for voltage tests at certain points in the circuit under test. The finished test probes are shown in Fig. 3.

WARNING: *Do not touch the tips of the probes on the continuity tester with the fingers when the tester is plugged into the power socket. Always handle by the taped part of the probe and unplug the tester when it is not actually in use.*

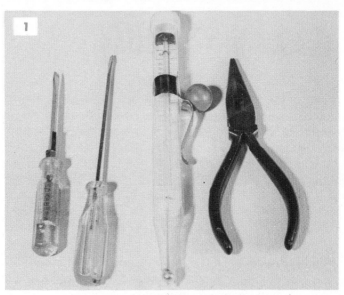

TESTING CORDS AND PLUGS

The cord of any electrical appliance is usually the part that fails first and is always the first thing to check in case of trouble. First examine the cord for any frayed spots in the covering, cracks in the insulation, or burned spots. If any of these symptoms are noted, replace the cord in all cases with a cord of the same type, or if the bad spot is near the plug, cut off the cord below the bad spot and replace the plug as shown in Fig. 4. Various types of replacement plugs are available at any hardware or electrical supply store (Fig. 5).

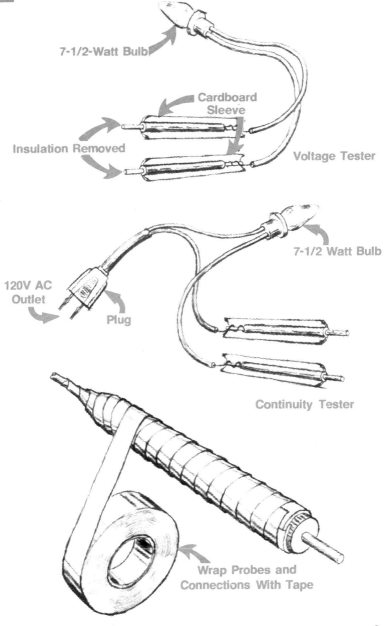

2

7-1/2-Watt Bulb

Cardboard Sleeve

Insulation Removed

Voltage Tester

120V AC Outlet

Plug

7-1/2 Watt Bulb

Continuity Tester

Wrap Probes and Connections With Tape

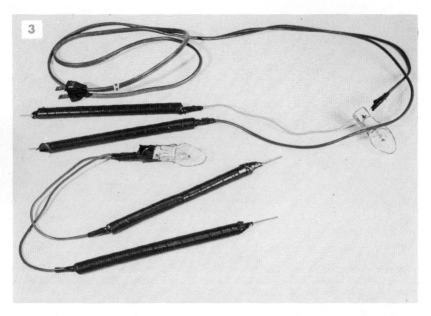

If the cord shows no visible signs of being bad, a simple test using both sets of the home-made probe testers can be made as follows:

Step 1. Plug in the *continuity tester.*

Step 2. Attach the probes of the continuity tester to the prongs of the plug on the cord under test. Most plugs have holes in the prongs and the tips of the probes can be placed in these holes to make contact. Be sure the two probe tips do not touch each other but are only in contact with the separate plug prongs.

Step 3. Place the probe tips of the voltage tester in contact with the two separate wires at the other end of the cord (Fig. 6). If the cord terminates in an appliance plug, simply insert the probe tips in the plug. If the cord does not have a plug at the appliance end, you will have to open the appliance and place the tips of the voltage tester on the connecting points of the cord that are inside the appliance as shown in Fig. 7.

4

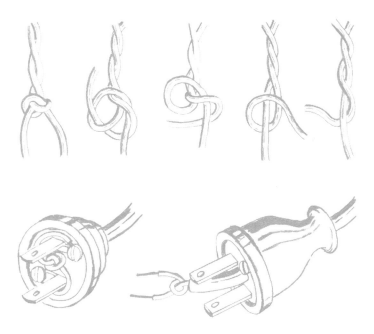

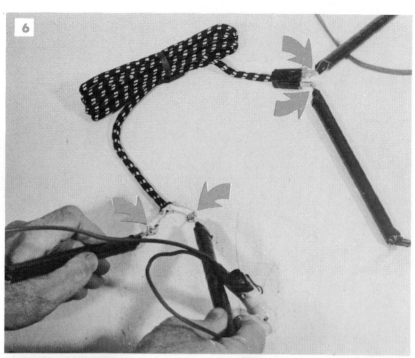

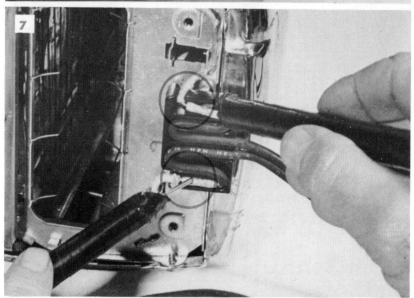

12

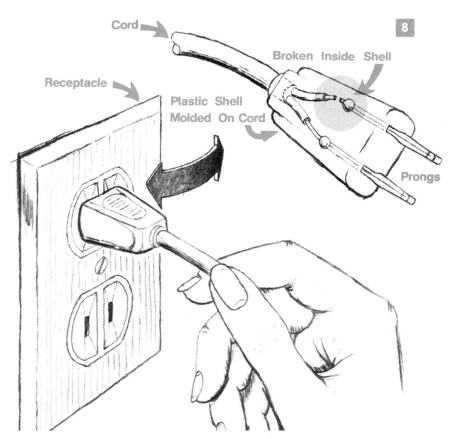

Cord

Receptacle

Plastic Shell Molded On Cord

Broken Inside Shell

Prongs

With the two sets of probes attached in this manner to each end of the cord, both lamps on the testers will light if the cord is in good condition. If only the continuity tester lamp glows, the cord is shorted and must be replaced. "Shorted" means that the insulation is broken on the cord in some manner that allows the two wires of the cord to touch each other. This condition usually causes some "fireworks" when the cord is plugged in and results in a blown house fuse.

If neither lamp is lit, the cord is open and also must be replaced unless the break is in the plug (**Fig.** 8) as is usually the case. Replacing the plug will solve this problem.

To replace the plug, first cut off the old plug with your pliers or a sharp knife; then put the end of the wire through the hole in the replacement plug so that the end comes out on the same side as the prongs. Now split the wire and pull the ends apart about 2 inches. With a knife, peel the insulation away from each wire about an inch. Twist the ends of each stranded wire together as shown in Fig. 9. Tie a simple overhand knot near the fork of the split and pull the knot back down into the plug. This will leave the two wires which are led one each around the outside of each prong and wrapped clockwise around the loosened connecting screws. See Fig. 4. Tighten the screws and the plug is ready for service.

If the cord is of the type that does not have an appliance plug at the other end but goes through the metal case of the appliance, the wire must be fed through the rubber or plastic strain-relief device to prevent electrical shorts to the case. Exact replacement cords usually have eyelets or push-on connectors on the appliance end. The eyelets are fastened under screws, much the same as the connections in a replacement plug. Fig. 10 shows the connection made inside an appliance of this type.

Heavy-duty connectors, called appliance plugs, are sometimes used at the appliance end of the cord. Some of these plugs are replaceable and are constructed as shown in Fig. 11. The ends of the two cord wires are stripped of insulation, twisted, and wrapped around the screws on the contacts in a clockwise direction. The screws are then tightened to make a solid connection. The plugs are wired in almost exactly the same manner as the replacement plug shown previously (Fig. 4). Other types of cords end in small solderless push-on connectors in which the wire is inserted and the connector is squeezed tight on the wire with pliers or a special crimping tool. After the plug (or plugs) is replaced, retest the cord as described in Steps 1 through 3.

A further test to be used on the repaired cord is shown in Fig. 12. A good cord will result in a lighted test lamp. If the lamp cannot be made to light in this test, your cord is not repaired yet and you must repeat the steps from the beginning until you find and repair the trouble.

9

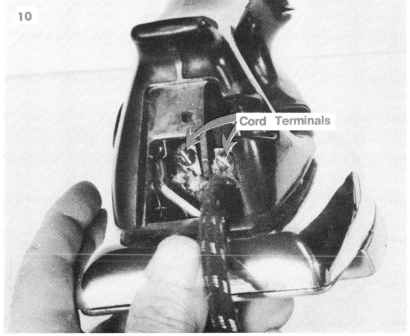

10

Cord Terminals

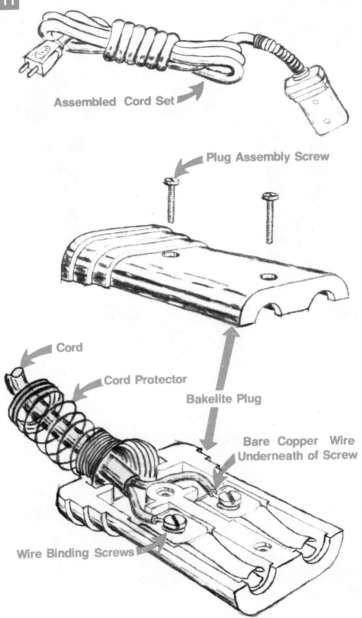

11

Assembled Cord Set

Plug Assembly Screw

Cord

Cord Protector

Bakelite Plug

Bare Copper Wire
Underneath of Screw

Wire Binding Screws

Exact replacement cords can be obtained at your local appliance service department (which you can find in the Yellow Pages of the phone book), or at most hardware or electrical supply stores. It is necessary to replace the cord with one of equal capacity because in heating-type appliances, if the cord is not heavy enough to take the current required, the cord will also heat along with the heating element and create a fire hazard.

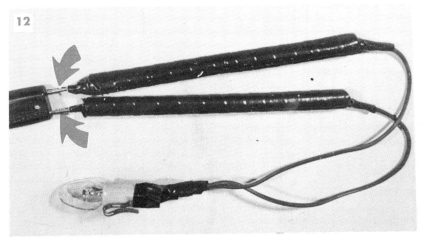

SWITCHES AND THERMOSTATS

Heating-type appliances consist basically of a line cord and heating element. In most circuits used today there are also included either a two or three contact switch, a thermostat, or in some cases, both a switch and a thermostat. The switch, shown schematically in Fig. 13, merely acts to close the circuit from the cord to the heating element or the thermostat. All heating circuits are continuous circuits. The continuous circuit of a heating-type appliance is shown in Fig 14.

Thermostats

Thermostats are another type of switch which are composed of blade-type springs with contacts which are joined when the thermostat is cold and separate when the temperature reaches a predetermined level.

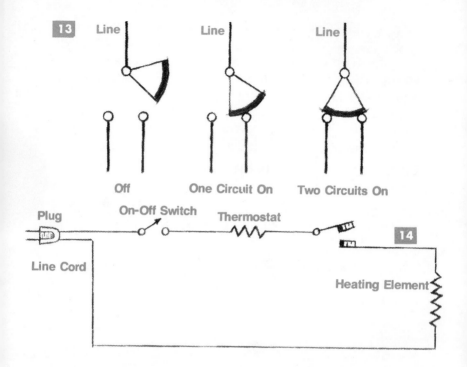

13

Line

Line

Line

Off   One Circuit On   Two Circuits On

Plug   On-Off Switch   Thermostat

14

Line Cord

Heating Element

The two blades of the thermostat are of different construction. The stationary blade is of ordinary spring steel
and the movable blade is made of two dissimilar metals
bonded together, which expand at different rates when
heated, thus causing the bimetal blade to bend away from
the stationary blade when heated. When the bimetal blade
bends far enough to open the contacts, the circuit is broken
and the heating element starts to cool. This in turn lets
the thermostat cool and the movable blade straightens
and comes back to make contact with the stationary blade,
again closing the circuit and starting the heating cycle
over again. Fig. 15 shows how the thermostat works. Thermostats in appliances are almost always adjustable (Fig. 16)
to vary the temperature at which they open and close.
In this way the temperature of the heating element in the
appliance is controlled. In some cases, toasters for example,
this temperature-controlling action of the thermostat is used

to time the cycle of heating. The thermostat in toasters usually has a separate heating coil at the thermostat connected in series with one of the toasting elements which causes the thermostat blade to work in a predetermined number of seconds and trip the pop-up mechanism at the same time the heating circuit is opened. This is the way your toast is made just the right shade.

Checking the Thermostats

The method in which a thermostat operates and also the test points are shown in Fig. 15. Points C and D are the two points at which the continuity probes should be connected to check for continuity. If the thermostat is closed, your test lamp should light when these two points are touched.

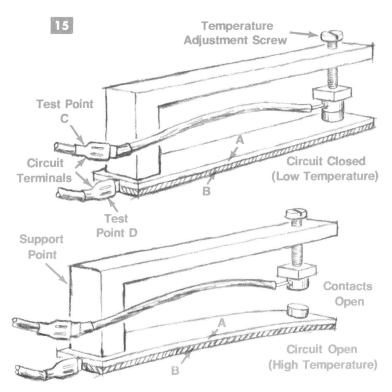

15

Temperature Adjustment Screw

Test Point C

Circuit Terminals

A

Circuit Closed (Low Temperature)

B

Test Point D

Support Point

Contacts Open

A

Circuit Open (High Temperature)

B

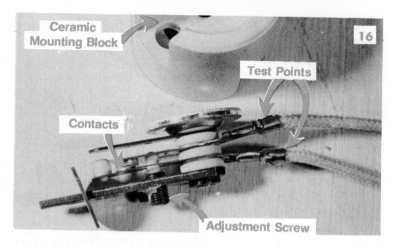

Ceramic Mounting Block

16

Test Points

Contacts

Adjustment Screw

Cleaning Thermostat Contacts

If the thermostat is closed and the continuity test lamp does not light, the contacts are probably dirty or corroded and should be cleaned. A small piece of very fine sandpaper should be inserted between the contact points and rubbed back and forth. If the sandpaper is folded, both contacts can be cleaned in one operation. After using the sandpaper, a card such as a postcard or business card should be inserted between the points and rubbed back and forth in the same manner as the sandpaper (Fig. 17). The card is just abrasive enough to impart a very smooth finish to the contacts.

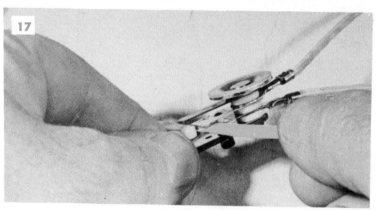

17

In some cases, the contacts will be so badly pitted that you will be unable to get them smooth. In that case, the thermostat will have to be replaced with an exact replacement unit. In the event that the thermostat is part of the appliance plug, it usually cannot be replaced, but the whole cord and control plug can be purchased at your appliance parts store.

As a final check, look at the thermostat carefully to make sure that the contacts touch tightly together when the thermostat is cold. If there is an adjustment screw on the contacts it can be turned until the contacts close. If there is no adjusting screw, the fixed blade, (not the bimetal blade) can sometimes be bent slightly to make the contacts close. This is a rather ticklish adjustment and may completely destroy the thermostat's usefulness unless done very carefully. The end result desired is for the contacts to barely close when the thermostat is cold and the contact points must meet squarely. If they touch only on one edge, you will have to clean the thermostat again after about a week of operation.

Many heating-type appliances have the thermostat control built into the appliance plug. The probe plug utilizes a heat probe which plugs into a socket in the base of the appliance and acts as a conductor of heat from the bottom of the skillet, grill, or other appliance, as the case may be, to the thermostat element in the plug proper. Fig. 18 shows a common type of probe plug with cover removed and the various parts indicated.

Fig. 19 shows a closeup view of the thermostat assembly in a probe plug. The repair and testing of probe-plug thermostats are the same as previously described for built-in thermostat controls. There are usually no adjustments that can be made to the probe plug thermostats except bending the adjusting tab up or down to vary the gap between the contact points on the thermostat blades.

HEATING ELEMENT

The one other part in the heating circuit of an appliance is the heating element. Heating elements are made in many different shapes and sizes but they are all essentially the

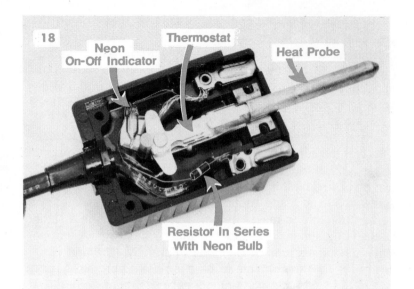

18

Neon
On-Off Indicator

Thermostat

Heat Probe

Resistor In Series
With Neon Bulb

same thing. They are made up of a resistance wire which gets extremely hot when current is passed through the element. The resistance wire is sometimes wound on mica sheets, wrapped around ceramic forms, or is embedded and completely sealed in some insulating heat-conducting material.

A schematic drawing of a heating circuit is shown in Fig. 14. You can see that all heating-type appliance circuits are series circuits which must have continuity to function. Heating elements can be tested separately by the use of the continuity tester as follows:

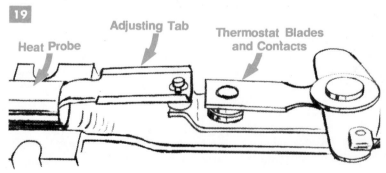

19

Adjusting Tab

Thermostat Blades
and Contacts

Heat Probe

22

Step 1. Locate the two end contacts of the heating element wires. Plug in the continuity tester.

Step 2. Place the continuity probes one on each end terminal of the resistance wire as shown in Fig. 20. The bulb will light if the element is not broken. If the bulb does not light, the resistance-wire heating element will have to be replaced with one of the same wattage rating.

Heating elements come in many different forms. There is no universal replacement but your local dealer or appliance store will have them in stock for the brands of appliance that they sell. You may, however, find universal replacements for the coil-wire type in an electrical supply store. The heaters come in different wattage ratings and must match the wattage rating of the element being replaced. The wattage necessary can be ascertained by reading the rating plate that you will find somewhere on the appliance. This plate will denote *total* wattage of the appliance. If the appliance has more than one element, divide the total wattage by the number of elements and this will give you the necessary wattage rating of one element. In the case of some space heaters which have fans, subtract about 30 watts from the total wattage rating. The difference will be the rating of the heating elements.

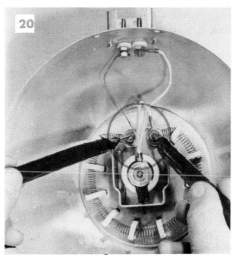

SECTION

Electric Toasters

The electric toaster is one of the oldest, and probably the most commonly used of electrical appliances. The basic toaster consists of a line cord connected to the heating element, or grids, which are arranged so that bread will be toasted when placed close to the elements. The heating elements consist of nichrome resistance wire wound on a mica form, although some toasters use coils of resistance wire for their heating elements.

AUTOMATIC TOASTERS

There is a great variety of automatic toasters on the market with somewhat different construction principles. In all cases, however, the heat from a heating element is used to toast the bread.

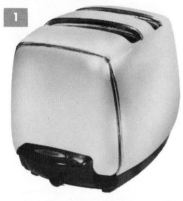

Most automatic toasters are the "Pop-up" type (Fig. 1) and include a thermostatic switch which controls the timing device. When the operating lever is pressed down, the thermostat is closed and the operating lever is latched in the down position. The closed thermostat closes the circuit to the heater coils which starts the cycle. The heat from the heater coils warms the thermostat causing it to bend in the manner described in Section 1. The bending of the thermostat blade in a period of time exerts pressure which unlatches the pop-up mechanism. The toast pops up and the electrical circuit to the heaters is opened.

TOASTER REPAIRS

The common complaint found with toasters is "no heat." No heating is usually caused by:
1. Loose toaster plug in wall socket.
2. Blown fuse in house circuit.
3. Defective wall outlet.
4. Defective cord.
5. Loose connections at terminals in plugs or in toaster.

If the toaster does not heat, the following steps should be followed to determine the cause.

Step 1. Use your voltage tester to check the wall socket as shown in Fig. 2. Insert the tips of the probes in the wall socket. If the bulb lights, the socket is in working condition. If the tester bulb does not light, the socket is either defective or the fuse in the house circuit is blown.

Step 2. Remove the bottom plate on the toaster. In some types, removing the bottom plate exposes the internal connections of the cord and the heating elements; in other types it is necessary to remove the entire case to reach the mechanism. Disassemble as far as is necessary to reach the connections as shown in Fig. 3.

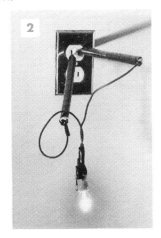

Step 3. Check the continuity of the line cord and plug by placing one probe tip of the continuity tester on one prong of the plug and the other probe on each of the internal connections of the cord in turn. You should get a continuity reading (tester bulb lit) on one of the connections. If you do not, the cord is open and must be replaced. If you get a lighted bulb on one connection, change your probes to the other plug prong and the other connection. A good plug and cord will show continuity with the probes in this position. See Fig. 4. If not, replace the cord according to instructions in Section 1.

Step 4. Do not plug in the toaster but push the lever down and latch it in the toast position. Look at the thermostat to make sure the contacts are closed.

Place your continuity tester with one probe on each of the internal cord connections. You will probably get no reading of continuity here since the toaster was not heating in the first place. Fig. 5 shows the probes on the internal cord connections.

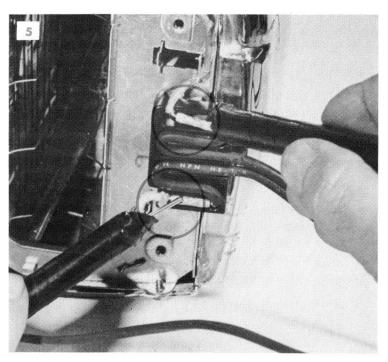

Step 5. Place continuity probes on the connections to
the heating elements. A reading of no continuity
(no light) here means your heating element
is open and must be replaced. Exact replacements for the heating elements can be purchased from your local service center or in most
electrical supply houses.

Step 6. If, in the test of Step 5, you *do* get a continuity
reading through the heating elements, either the
thermostatic switch is defective or the thermostat-heating element is open. Examine the thermostat contacts to be sure they are closed and
making good contact. Clean them as described
in Section 1. If they are not closed, turn the
adjusting screw (or nut) until the contacts close.
This adjustment screw is sometimes the "Light-
Dark" adjustment and can be turned in by re-

29

moving the plastic knob on the adjustment, turning the screw in the direction of darker, and replacing the knob in a slightly different position on the shaft. If closing the contacts does not activate the heating elements, the thermostat-heating element is defective. This will usually involve changing the entire thermostat unit. The old element must be removed by loosening the screws or rivets that hold it in place and disconnecting the wires leading to the thermostat unit. Replace with a new unit in exactly the same position and with the connecting wires connected the same as was the old unit. If the unit was installed with rivets in the original, the rivets can be replaced by small machine bolts or metal screws.

Step 7. When you have completed repairs, plug the toaster cord into the wall socket and depress the carriage lever to a latched position. This should turn on the toaster. The "on time" can be adjusted by the thermostat adjustment screw as described in Step 6. The mechanical parts of the latching and pop-up mechanism should be cleaned to make sure they operate freely. This is a mechanical operation and all parts should operate easily and they may need to be lubricated sparingly with silicon grease. The toaster should be tested by actually toasting bread and adjusting the thermostat adjustment to the position where the bread is toasted to the desired shade. The "Light-Dark" lever or knob should be set at the middle position to allow a range of lighter or darker when the toaster is put back in service. With any given adjustment of the thermostat, the toast will be lighter on the second and succeeding slices of bread because the thermostat blade is already warm and is partially bent, thus, it will not have so far to move to trip the carriage latch.

Another toaster with a slightly different pop-up control mechanism is shown in Fig. 6. The line cord continuity tests can be made on this model by removing a small bakelite cover (Fig. 7) on the bottom of the toaster. The removal of this cover, which also acts as a strain relief for the cord, permits the removal of the cord as shown in Fig. 8. The cord is attached by solderless push-on terminals which are removed allowing the cord to be tested for continuity before disassembling the toaster proper.

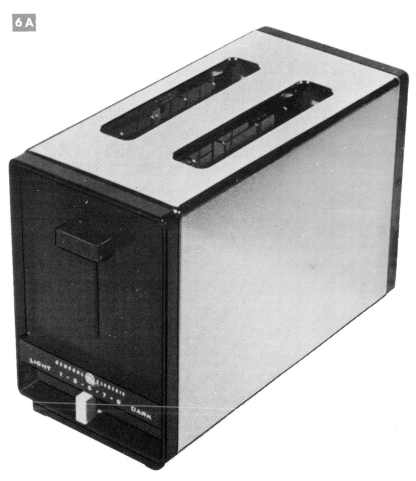

6 A

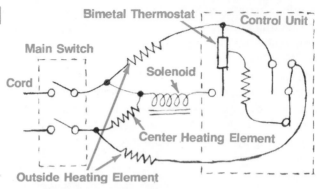

6 B

Bimetal Thermostat

Control Unit

Main Switch

Cord

Solenoid

Center Heating Element

Outside Heating Element

7

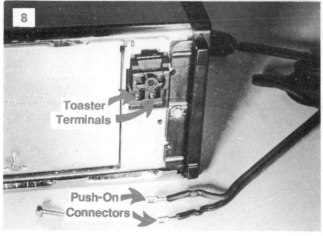

8

Toaster
Terminals

Push-On
Connectors

No Heat Symptom

Step 1. Remove the cord and test for continuity as described in Section 1. If the cord shows no continuity, replace with an exact replacement cord, or if the cord is broken or burned near the plug, replace plug with a replacement plug and retest cord for continuity.

Step 2. Push the bread carriage lever down until it latches. Use your continuity tester and apply the probe tips, one to each contact, to the line cord contacts as shown in Fig. 9. An open circuit reading here (no light) can indicate that the main switch is defective, and require further disassembly and testing.

Step 3. Remove the "Light-Dark" switch knob and the bread carriage knob by pulling straight out on the knobs as shown in Fig. 10. Now remove the two hex-head screws at each end of the bottom plate. The two bakelite end pieces of the case can now be pulled off as shown in Fig. 11, and the metal cover can be removed by carefully lifting straight up.

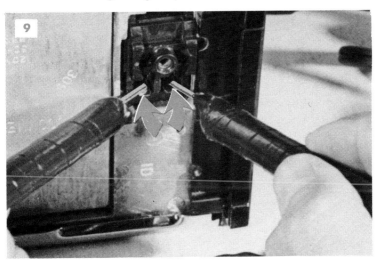

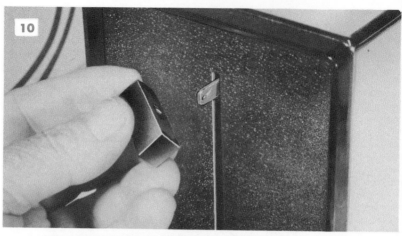

Step 4. Check to make sure that when the bread-carriage lever is depressed and locked that it also depresses the switch arm as shown in Fig. 12. Release the bread-carriage latch and allow the carriage to pop up. Apply the probes of the continuity tester to the two terminals on top of the switch as shown in Fig. 13. Continuity at this point and no continuity at the cord terminals (Fig. 9) indicates that the switch is bad and will have to be replaced. The switch can be removed by cutting the wires attached

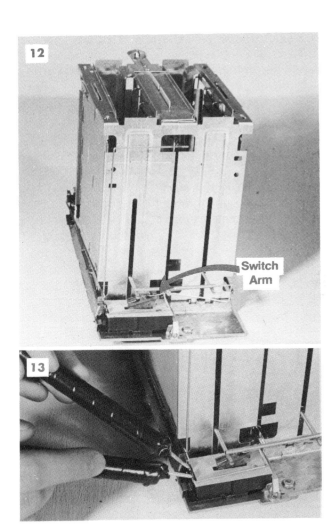

to the terminals, removing a small spring clip at the end of the switch assembly and lifting out the switch unit. On replacing the unit with an exact replacement, the terminals must be silver-soldered to the old wires on the toaster. Also, the heating elements must be silver-soldered when replaced. This limits the possible repairs of this toaster to the average homeowner.

TOASTER LATCHING TROUBLES

In some cases the complaint will be "bread carriage will not latch down" or "toast does not pop up." For these troubles go to the control-unit end of the toaster and perform the following tests and repairs.

Won't Stay Down

Check the latch at the top of the solenoid coil (Fig. 14). It may be bent and cannot latch the carriage. Also check the cool-down adjustment screw (Fig. 15). It should not be touching the thermostat spring when the carriage bar is first depressed. Use your small screwdriver and turn the screw counterclockwise until it opens. If the carriage will still not lock down, use your pliers to adjust the latch to a position where it locks.

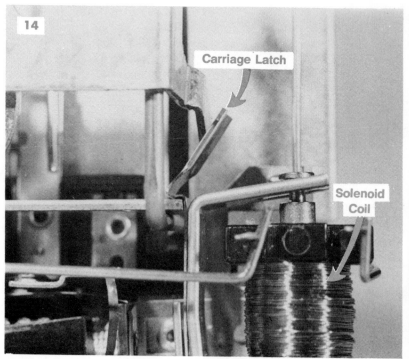

Carriage Latch

Solenoid Coil

Adjustment Screw

Won't Pop Up

Do not plug toaster into the electric socket. Use the continuity tester to check the solenoid coil as shown in Fig. 16. If no continuity is read across the solenoid (no light on tester), the entire control unit will have to be replaced by an exact replacement from the manufacturer. However, if the solenoid shows continuity, plug in the toaster and depress the carriage until it latches. Turn the cool down adjustment in a clockwise direction until the screw makes contact with the thermostat blade after allowing the toaster to heat for a short while. The latch should release as soon as the screw touches the thermostat blade. If the latch does not release when adjusted in this manner, the thermostat bimetal unit is bad and the entire control unit must be replaced. Here again, the unit must be silver-soldered in place and if you cannot perform silver-soldering, no repairs are possible.

Toast Too Light or Too Dark

Plug in toaster, insert a slice of bread, and depress and latch-in on the carriage. If toast is too light, turn the cool-down adjustment counterclockwise one full turn and test with a slice of bread. If toast is too dark, turn cool-down adjustment screw one half turn clockwise and test. Adjust and readjust this screw until bread is toasted the desired amount. Make these adjustments with the "Light-Dark" lever in a middle position. Turning the adjusting screw one half turn usually varies the toasting time several seconds so the adjustment will have to be very gradual, testing with a fresh slice of bread after every adjustment.

REASSEMBLY

Reassembly is the opposite of disassembly.

Step 1. Place metal cover over the toaster unit.

Step 2. Replace the end piece opposite the controls and fit the lugs on the bakelite end piece into the slots in the end of the metal cover. Insert the hex-head screw in the bottom of the end piece but do not tighten completely.

Step 3. Put the control-end piece on, carefully aligning control levers in the slots. Squeeze together on the two end pieces and insert the hex-head screw into the bottom at the control end of the toaster. Tighten both hex-head screws.

Step 4. Push control knobs in place.

SECTION

Electric Irons

Electric irons actually contain a very simple electrical circuit. They consist of a heating element, a thermostat, and a line cord. An older model automatic iron is shown in Fig. 1.

The heating elements consist of nichrome resistance wire wound on special mica forms or spiral coils in a special metal tube which is an integral part of the sole plate of the iron. The heating element must be insulated from the sole plate.

Electric irons may be conveniently classified as:

1. Automatic irons.
2. Automatic steam irons.

AUTOMATIC IRONS

Automatic irons include a heat control device, or thermostat. The thermostat regulates the heat to a specific value determined by the setting of the temperature control. The thermostat contacts are closed when the iron is turned on, and when the temperature of the sole plate (and the thermostat) becomes sufficiently high, the thermostat contacts open and the iron begins to cool. When the iron reaches a lower temperature, the thermostat contacts close and the cycle is repeated. In this way, the temperature of the sole plate is held nearly constant.

The automatic iron is equipped with a heat-control knob which is mounted on the handle. The knob is coupled through a small shaft to a cam arrangement on the thermostat (Fig. 2) that varies the setting of the thermostat blade when the control knob is rotated. In this way, different temperature settings are obtained for ironing different types of fabrics.

Complaints with the automatic iron usually are:

1. No heat.
2. Heat too low.
3. Heat too high.

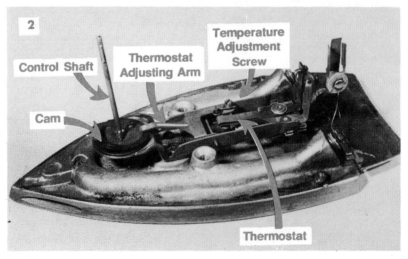

Heat Too High or Too Low

If the complaint is "heat too high or too low," an adjustment of the thermostat heat control is required. You can use the "cut-and-try" method of heat adjustment or you can use your thermometer and set up a test stand to test the temperature. A test stand can be made as shown in Fig. 3. The iron can be placed on a couple of pieces of heat insulating material, such as pieces of ceramic tile, in a way that the tip of your thermometer can be placed under the pointed tip of the sole plate. The thermometer bulb must be in contact with the sole plate.

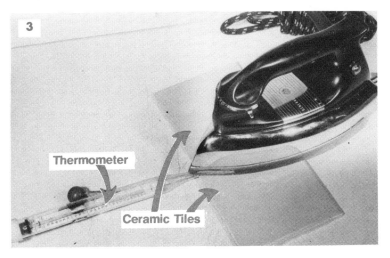

Step 1. Remove the saddle plate on the top of the iron as shown in Fig. 4. This exposes a hole in the shell of the iron, under which the temperature adjustment screw will be found.

Step 2. Insert a small screwdriver through the hole (Fig. 5) and engage the adjusting-screw slot. Turn the adjustment screw clockwise to decrease temperature or counterclockwise to increase temperature. A very small movement of the adjusting screw changes the temperature several degrees so don't overdo the adjustment.

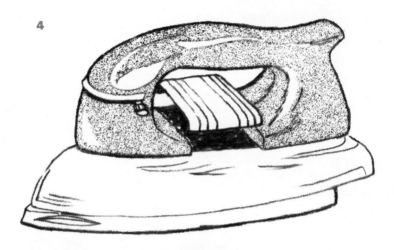

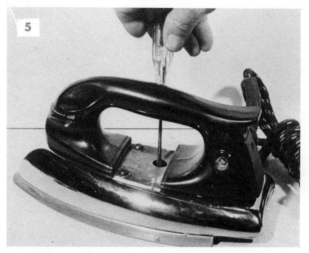

Step 3. Plug in the iron and set the control knob to the "wool" position. The temperature of the sole plate should rise to approximately 340 degrees, plus or minus 35 degrees. The temperature should go up and down between this point and not more than 50 degrees lower as the thermostat switches off and on regulating the temperature.

Step 4. Turn the control knob on the handle to maximum temperature and retest. The temperature at maximum setting should not rise to more than 465 degrees, plus or minus 50 degrees. If the temperature varies from this point, readjust the temperature adjusting screw as instructed in Step 2. These adjustments may have to be made several times before the proper temperature ranges are obtained.

No-Heat Symptom

If the iron fails to heat at all, the trouble is usually one of three things:

1. Faulty cord or wall outlet.
2. Dirty or corroded thermostat contacts.
3. Open heating element.

Step 1. Remove the cover plate on the rear of the iron (Fig. 6) and locate the terminals to which the cord connects (Fig. 7). Plug in your continuity tester and test the probe set by touching the probe tips together. Test lamp should light. Now place probe tips one on each of the cord plug prongs and turn the iron heat-control knob to an "on" position. If the iron and cord are in good

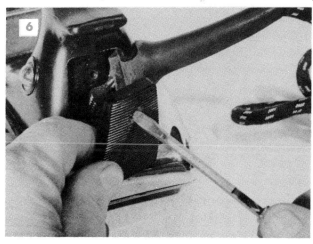

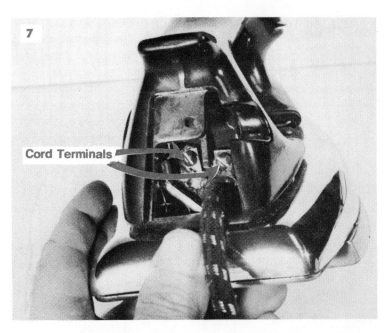

7

Cord Terminals

condition, you should have a continuity indication (test lamp lighted) at this point. Since the
iron was not heating, you will probably get an
open indication. The exception would be if the
cord were shorted and in this case you would
have blown fuses in the house circuit when you
attempted to use the iron. If this occurs, the cord
will obviously have to be changed.

Step 2. Place the probe tips on the two terminals inside
the iron as shown in Fig. 8. A continuity reading
here (test lamp lighted) indicates that the iron
is operating but the cord is bad (open) and must
be replaced. Remove the terminal screws and
slip the cord and the rubber protective sleeve
out of the iron. Obtain an electric-iron replacement cord from your local hardware or electrical
supply store and replace in the iron exactly as
it originally was installed. Plug in the iron cord
and test to see if the iron heats.

Step 3. If no continuity reading is obtained in Step 2, the trouble lies in the thermostat or in the heating element. This requires further disassembly of the iron and herein sometimes lies a problem.

There are many variations in the construction of electric irons and it is impossible to give specific data on disassembling your iron. Two general rules should be followed however: there will always be an easy way to disassemble the iron—the trick is to find it. First take out all visible screws and fastenings; if the iron does not come apart, look for some hidden key or trigger which will release the rest of the parts. The other rule is *never* use force. Although the temptation may be great, resist it. Using force will only damage some part which may be difficult to replace. An iron with the top shell and handle removed is shown in Fig. 9.

Step 4. Plug in your continuity test set. Place the probes on the heating element terminals as shown in Fig. 10. A "continuity" reading here indicates that the heating element is in operating condition and the trouble is in the thermostat switch. A "no continuity" reading (test lamp not lit) indicates a defective heating element and the iron is not repairable. The heating element is sealed in the sole plate and a new sole plate is not available as a repair part. The entire iron must be discarded.

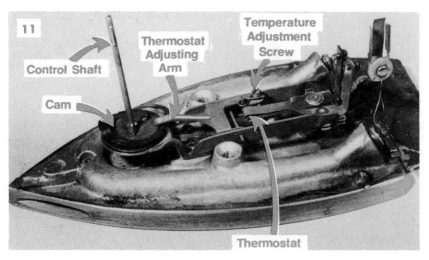

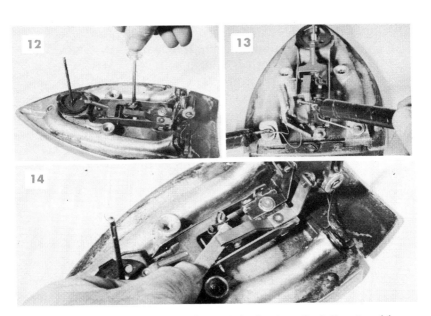

Step 5. If the test of Step 4 indicates that the trouble
is in the thermostat (Fig. 11) inspect the thermostat and make sure the contact points are closed
when the heat-control is in the "On" position. If
the points are not closed, carefully adjust the
heat-adjustment screw (Fig. 12) until the points
close. Note that one of the thermostat connecting terminals is connected directly (by a wire) to
one terminal of the heating element. Place one
of the continuity probes on the thermostat
terminal that is *not* connected to the heating element and the other probe tip on the connected
heating-element terminal as shown in Fig. 13.
If thermostat points are closed, you should get
a "continuity" reading at these points. If not,
clean the thermostat points with a small piece
of fine sandpaper (Fig. 14) and burnish with a
small strip of cardboard as described in Section
1 of this book. Retest for continuity as shown
in Fig. 13. If you do not have continuity, the
thermostat is defective and must be replaced.

Step 6. To remove the thermostat, remove the screws from the thermostat terminals. Now remove the screws which hold the thermostat to the sole plate of the iron (Fig. 15) and lift out the thermostat unit (Fig. 16). Replace with an exact replacement thermostat which can be obtained from the manufacturer's service department. Reassemble the thermostat and the balance of the iron and adjust temperature as previously described in this section. Your iron is now repaired.

Step 7. As a final test, plug in the continuity tester. Place one probe tip on the metal shell of the iron and the other probe tip on each of the prongs of the cord plug (Fig. 17). The control knob on the iron should be placed in one of the "On" positions for this test. If the lamp in the tester lights, the indication is that a short to the shell exists somewhere in the heater circuit. This is a dangerous condition and the short must be located and repaired before placing the iron in service.

15

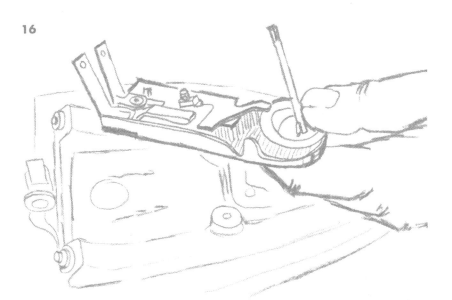

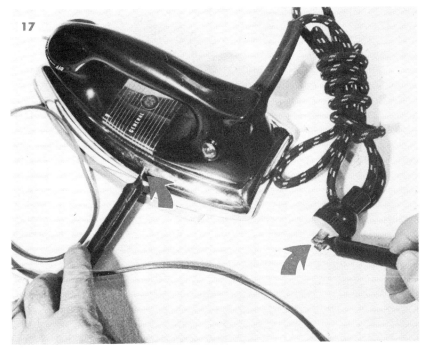

AUTOMATIC STEAM IRONS

Steam irons differ from automatic irons mainly in that they require special care and maintenance because of their water and steam reservoirs. The steam system requires that gaskets be tight to prevent water and steam leaks, and valves should be cleaned periodically to remove scale. There will, however, be little trouble with the steam system if distilled water is always used.

An example of a modern automatic steam-or-dry iron is shown in Fig. 18. Electrically, the iron is identical to the automatic iron described previously. The electrical circuit consists of a cord, thermostat, and a heating element cast into the sole plate of the iron.

In addition, the iron contains a water tank, a needle valve to control the flow of water into the water tank, and a small plunger-type pump which injects water into the steam chamber.

The system uses a flash-type steam generating system. The steam chamber is directly over the sole plate and water is injected onto the hot sole plate where it immediately becomes steam. The pressure of the steam in the steam chamber forces the steam out through the outlets in the bottom of the sole plate into the fabric being pressed. A view of the partly disassembled iron is shown in Fig. 19.

18

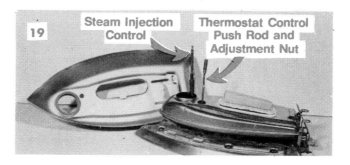

ELECTRICAL REPAIRS

The usual complaints regarding steam irons are the same as the automatic iron. They are:

1. No heat.
2. Too high heat. (Causes sputtering or ejection of water from steam ports.)
3. Too low heat. (Iron does not steam.)

Too High or Too Low Heat

Step 1. Check the operating temperature of the iron with the test setup described previously for automatic irons. Depending on the type iron, temperature adjustments will vary. In the particular iron described here, the temperature adjustment is a nut at the top of the temperature-control push rod. It will be necessary to remove the handle and control assembly from the iron in order to get at the adjusting nut (Fig. 19). Disassembly, as always, may pose problems. Remove all the screws you can find and look for the hidden catch that releases the handle. In this iron, it is a small plastic pin located in the top of the handle just under the steam injector button. Drive the plastic pin *into* the handle. It will be recovered later after you remove the handle. *Do not try to pull it out.* A view of the iron with the handle assembly removed is shown in Fig. 20.

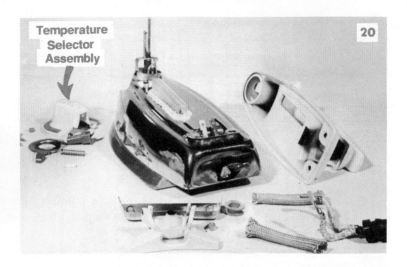

20

Temperature Selector Assembly

Step 2. To adjust the temperature, it is necessary to turn the nut at the top of the control push rod shown in Fig. 20. Turning the nut counterclockwise, as you look down on the iron, increases the operating temperature; clockwise decreases the temperature. After making an adjustment, it will be necessary to reinstall the handle to test for proper temperature. The maximum sole-plate temperature should be 455 degrees plus or minus 50 degrees. After adjustment, be sure that the iron shuts off with the temperature control knob in the "Off" position. If it does not, it will be necessary to readjust the push rod nut in a clockwise direction until the iron shuts off in the "Off" position.

No Heat

No-heat problems are checked in exactly the same manner as with the automatic iron described previously.

Step 1. Check the cord for continuity in the same manner as before and check the wall outlet for voltage. Replace cord if necessary.

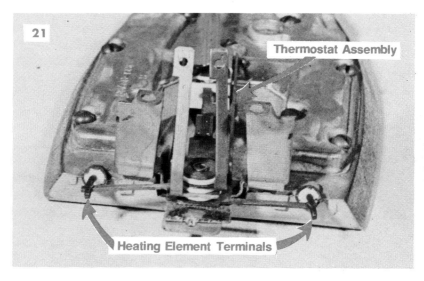

Thermostat Assembly

Heating Element Terminals

Step 2. If the cord is in good condition, continue dis-assembly of the iron by removing the shell and the water tank. The sole plate and thermostat assembly is shown in Fig. 21 with the tank and shell removed.

Step 3. Check the heating element for continuity by placing the continuity-tester probes on the terminals at the rear of the sole plate as shown in the previous section on automatic irons (Fig. 10). If continuity is indicated, the heating element is good. If there is no continuity (lamp in tester not lit), no further repairs are possible since the heating element is sealed in the sole plate.

Step 4. If the heating element checked OK in Step 3, place the continuity probes on the two cord terminals as shown in Fig. 22. Press down the thermostat control lever to close the thermo-stat contacts (Figs. 22 and 23). You should get a continuity reading. If the reading indicates "no continuity," the thermostat is defective or the contact points are dirty and corroded.

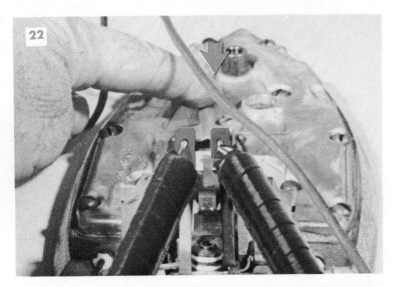

Step 5. Clean contact points, if indicated by the previous test, with fine sandpaper and burnish with a piece of cardboard. Repeat the test of Step 4. If you still have no continuity, the thermostat must be replaced. Thermostat replacement generally follows the same procedure as shown in the previous section on Automatic Irons.

Reassembly after repairs is accomplished in the reverse manner from disassembly and varies with different brands of irons. After reassembly, test the iron for proper temperature control as described before. Make any necessary adjustments.

STEAM SYSTEM PROBLEMS

In addition to the electrical problems, automatic steam irons may have steaming difficulties. Some complaints with the steam system are:

1. Won't steam or insufficient steam.
2. Sputters or spits water from steam ports.
3. Spots material.
4. Burns holes in clothes.

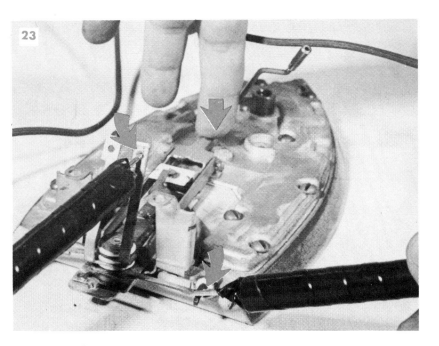

Won't Steam

This condition usually indicates that the iron has been used with hard water and the steam passages are completely or partially clogged. Clean steam ports with a stiff wire. Run a tank full of special steam-iron cleaner through the iron.

Sputters or Spits Water

This symptom usually indicates that the iron is operating at an excessively high temperature. Check the temperature and adjust as described previously.

Spots Material

Complaints of brown spots usually means that charred inorganic material has worked its way into the steam chamber or steam passages. Fill and flood the sole plate steam chamber with water by operating the steam-control pump button while the iron is cold. Then turn the iron on "steam" and allow the water to boil out through the steam ports. The boiling water will flush the brown material from the iron. Repeat this operation if necessary.

Burns Holes in Clothes

Complaints that steam irons burn holes in clothes can usually be traced to buying distilled water from service stations where the water contains traces of sulphuric battery acid. Use only *pure* distilled water in the iron.

Electric Skillets

The electric skillet (Fig. 1) is a cooking pan with a built-in electric heating element which is actually a part of the skillet. The thermostat control is built into a large appliance plug and contains a large prong which fits into a recess in the skillet bottom. This large prong conducts heat from the skillet bottom to the thermostat control and acts as a thermostat heater. When the thermostat bimetallic blade is heated to the temperature of the heat probe, the thermostat opens until such time as the skillet bottom drops to a cooler

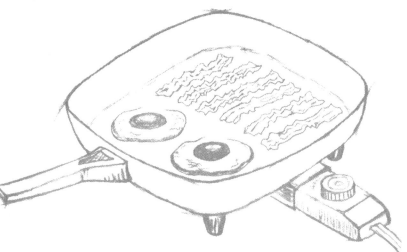

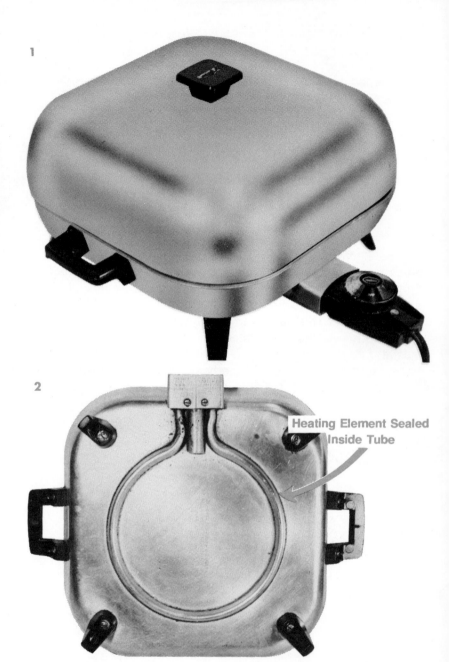

1

2

Heating Element Sealed Inside Tube

temperature whereupon the thermostat closes and begins the heating cycle again. This process maintains the temperature of the skillet within a limited temperature range, which is governed by the setting of the thermostat temperature-control knob on the plug. The range between thermostat "on" and thermostat "off" is about 40°F. In some types of electric skillets, the thermostats and controls are built into the handle. In this type, the handle cannot be immersed in water during the washing of the skillet because liquids will damage the thermostat.

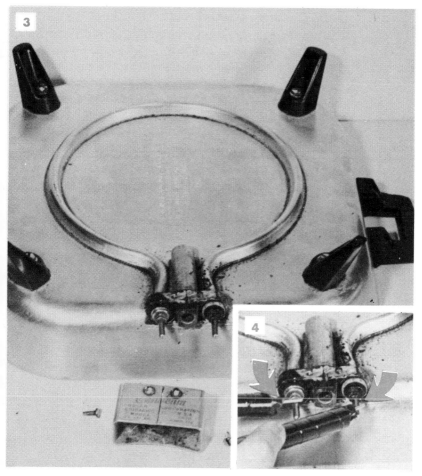

SKILLET DOES NOT HEAT

There are no repairs that can be made to the skillet proper. The heating element (the raised circular ridge on the bottom of the skillet) is sealed into the bottom of the skillet as shown in Fig. 2. However, a test should be made of the heating element for continuity to find out immediately if the skillet can be repaired or must be discarded.

Step 1. Turn the skillet bottom side up and remove the guard over the heating element prongs (Fig. 3).

Step 2. Plug in your continuity tester. Touch the two probe tips together to see if the tester is working. If it is, the bulb will light. Place one probe tip on one prong and the other probe tip on the other prong as shown in Fig. 4. If the bulb lights in the tester, there is probably no trouble with the heating element and further tests will have to be made to the cord and thermostat control

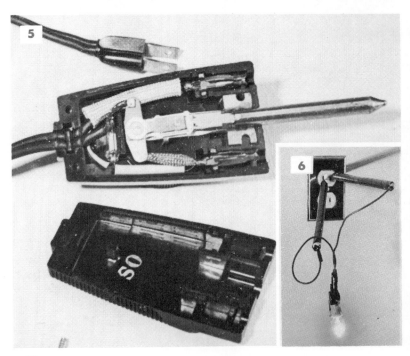

plug. If the lamp in the tester does not light, the heating element is open and the skillet is not repairable.

If the heating element shows continuity, the trouble must be in the cord or the thermostat-probe plug and the following steps are in order:

Step 1. Examine the cord carefully for any burned or frayed spots in the insulation. It will be necessary to take the probe plug apart to check continuity in the cord and plug (Fig. 5). You will find that one wire of the cord goes directly to one plug contact and the other cord wire is connected to the thermostat. With the plug switch in the "Off" position, plug the cord into a live wall outlet. Check the outlet with your voltage tester as shown in Fig. 6 before plugging in the cord. Be very careful not to touch any of the internal connections with your fingers, any metal object, or anything except your test-probe handles. You could receive a bad shock if you touch a live contact.

Step 2. Place the tips of the voltage tester on the points to which the line cord connects as shown in Fig. 7. If the test lamp lights, the cord and the wall plug are operating satisfactorily. If the lamp does not light, the cord will have to be replaced, or possibly only the line plug.

Step 3. If the cord checks OK, turn the thermostat control knob to the "On" position and place one probe tip in each of the contacts which plug into the skillet as shown in Fig. 8. If the lamp lights, everything is OK and you have no trouble in the thermostat. However, if an "Open" reading is indicated (no light) the thermostat is not making connection. Visually inspect the contacts on the thermostat to see if they are closed. If the contacts are closed, and you still get no light on the tester, unplug the cord and clean the thermostat contacts with a piece of fine

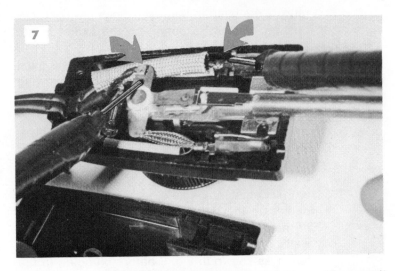

sandpaper and finish the burnishing with a small strip of cardboard as shown in Fig. 9. Plug in the cord and retest at the plug terminals as shown in Fig. 8. The lamp should now light unless the thermostat is defective.

Step 4. The thermostat contact points should be open when the temperature selector knob is turned to the "Off" position, and should close as soon as the knob is turned to the first calibrating mark on the dial. Examine the points (with the cord unplugged from the wall outlet) to see if they open and close with the movement of the dial to "Off" and "On." If they do not close and open properly, the blade of the thermostat can be bent, very carefully, to a position where the contacts open and close at the proper position of the switch. This is a very "ticklish" repair and is seldom successful without completely destroying the proper operation of the temperature control. However, it is worth trying if the control is not working at all, because if the bending is not successful, a new control plug will have to be purchased anyway. If you have to replace

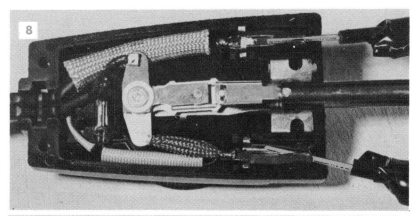

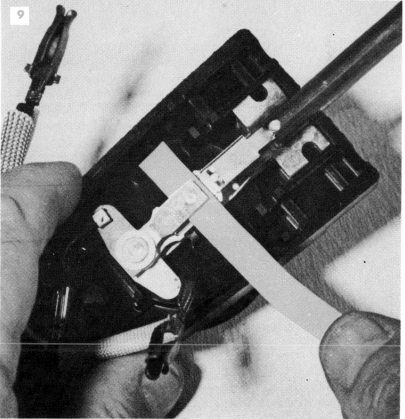

the cord, the end connectors in the control plug are usually made to solderless connections, either screws or the squeeze type connector. If they are of the squeeze type, you can open them by inserting some sharp pointed tool in the connector and prying them open. The new cord ends, after being stripped of insulation of about a half inch, can then be inserted in the connector and the connector squeezed together to form a tight connection.

The thermostat plug usually also contains a small neon light and series resistor (Fig. 10) wired across the plug terminals. If the skillet is working and the bulb doesn't light when the skillet is on, this bulb will have to be replaced. Make sure all leads inside the plug are properly placed and with all insulating sleeves in place before replacing the plug cover.

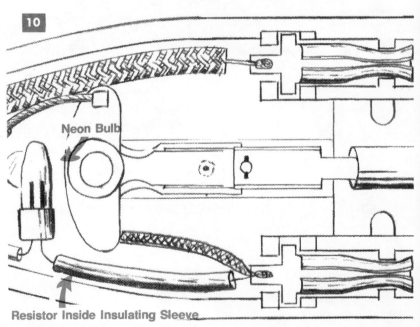

10

Neon Bulb

Resistor Inside Insulating Sleeve

Step 5. As a final safety test, plug in your continuity tester and plug the control-plug into the skillet. Turn the temperature knob to the "On" position. Place one probe of the continuity tester on the bare metal of the skillet and the other probe on the line cord plug terminals as shown in Fig. 11. If the light on your continuity tester lights you have not properly replaced the wires in the control plug and one of them is shorted to the heat-sensor plug or the heating element is shorted to the skillet proper inside the skillet. In either case, a dangerous condition exists and the skillet should be discarded or the plug reinspected and repaired to eliminate the short.

Step 6. After the skillet is repaired, you may want to make a temperature check. Put about ½ inch of cold water in the skillet and set the thermostat at around 200 degrees. Place a candy thermometer in position so that the tip is approxi-

mately in the middle of the skillet. If the thermostat is adjusted properly, the heat should be shut off (pilot light out) at the time the thermometer indicates between 200 and 220 degrees. The skillet will then cool down somewhat and the thermostat should close again at a temperature of between 180 and 200 degrees. If the on-off temperatures fall within this range, the thermostat and skillet are in perfect working order.

SECTION

Coffee Makers

All electric coffee makers have an electric heating element fitted into the base, a thermostat, and in most types, a removable cord set with an appliance plug. Coffee makers may generally be classified into two types: the brewer-type and the percolator.

BREWER-TYPE COFFEE MAKER

A fully automatic electric coffee maker of the brewer-type is shown in Fig. 1. To better understand the mechanism and heating circuit, a drawing is shown in Fig. 2. The heating element, switch, and thermostat are fitted on the bottom of the lower bowl inside a bakelite base.

Due to the slightly complicated thermostat switching used in this type coffee maker, an explanation of the operating cycle is necessary. Refer to Fig. 2. Electric current enters at the terminal post, passes through the heating element into the low-heat contact spring, through the silver contact points, into the terminal contact spring, thus completing the circuit back to the other terminal post. This circuit is exactly the same on either the high-heat or low-heat position. The only change is a mechanical one which changes the position of the terminal contact spring by means of the high-low switch.

1

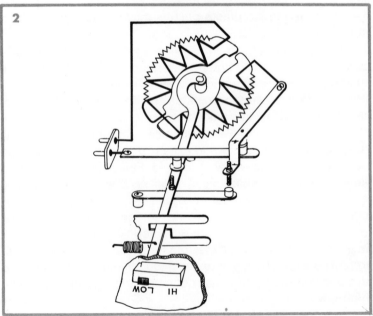

When the switch is in the "low" position (as shown in Fig. 2) and the cord is plugged in, the heating element is heated and in turn heats the bimetal thermostat blade. When the water in the pot (and the thermostat blade) reaches a temperature of approximately 185 degrees, the thermostat opens the contact points and the water cools, thus cooling the thermostat. When the temperature drops to approximately 165 degrees, the thermostat closes the contact points and the heating cycle commences again. If the low-heat adjustment screw is adjusted properly, the temperature of the water in the pot will remain within these limits which is not hot enough to rise to the upper bowl.

To make coffee, the switch is set in the "high" position which puts the switch arm into the step on the switch bracket where it is held by a spring. This brings the high-heat adjustment screw closer to the thermostat blade. At the same time, the ceramic slide button will come under projection "X" (shown in Fig. 2), thus pushing both the springs and the adjusting screw away from the thermostat blade and closing the silver switch contacts. The current passing through the heating element causes the temperature of the thermostat to rise. The thermostat blade, on reaching a high temperature when the water is all driven up into the upper bowl, bends and pushes the switch lever out of the step in the switch bracket and the spring pulls it back into the lower position. When this occurs, the low-heat adjustment screw is immediately pushed by the thermostat blade, thus opening the silver switch contacts. The contacts remain open until enough heat is lost to permit the thermostat to close the contacts to initiate the low-heat cycle described previously.

One of the features of this coffee maker is that the water rising to the upper bowl only reaches a temperature of slightly more than 200 degrees, which is claimed to be the best temperature for brewing coffee. When the water has reached the proper temperature and goes up to the upper bowl, all but a very small quantity boils away and the steam agitates the coffee in the upper bowl. When all water is out of the lower bowl, the heat increases rapidly causing the thermostat to kick the switch off the step on the switch bracket into the "low" position. As the temperature decreases, a partial vacuum is produced in the lower bowl and the coffee is forced down through the filter into the lower bowl where it is kept at a temperature of between 165 and 185 degrees by the low-heat setting of the thermostat.

The usual complaints with the brewer-type coffee maker are:

1. Water does not all rise to upper bowl before high heat cuts off.
2. Coffee maker heats water but water does not rise at all.
3. Water rises but thermostat does not shut off high heat.
4. Water all rises to upper bowl but coffee does not go back (or is slow to go back) to lower bowl.
5. Coffee maker does not heat at all.

Water Does Not Rise

If the complaint is "water does not rise before high heat cuts off," the trouble is probably that the high-heat adjustment is off. Proceed with the following steps to adjust the thermostat.

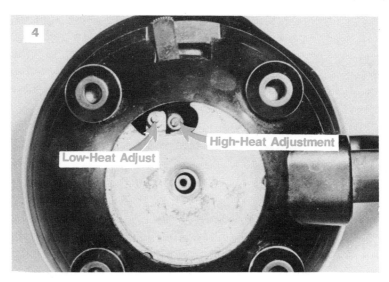

4

Low-Heat Adjust

High-Heat Adjustment

Step 1. Remove the screw in the circular bottom rating plate of the base and lift out the plate as shown in Fig. 3. An oblong opening in the bottom retaining plate will be exposed. Two adjustment screws will be visible (Fig. 4). With the coffee maker upside down looking down in the opening, the adjustment screw that is deepest is the "high-heat" adjustment. Loosen the locking nut with your long-nose pliers and turn the adjusting screw about one full turn counterclockwise. The counterclockwise direction increases the high-heating time; turning the screw in a clockwise direction decreases the "high-heat" time.

Step 2. Fill the lower bowl with water, insert the upper bowl and put the filter in place. Plug in the cord and set the switch in the high position. Observe whether all the water rises to the upper bowl before the switch snaps into "low" position. If the cycle is not satisfactory, empty the pot and re-adjust the high-heat adjusting screw, counterclockwise to increase the high-heat time and clockwise to decrease it. You may have to repeat the foregoing test and adjustment several times to get it right. Start the cycle with cool water each time you test the cycle. When the adjustment is reached that is satisfactory, retighten the lock nut on the adjustment screw without moving the adjustment screw itself.

Water Heats But Does Not Rise

This symptom may be caused by a leaking bowl gasket (Fig. 5) or wrong adjustment of the "low-heat" adjustment screw.

Step 1. Inspect the bowl gasket to see if it is seating into the bowl tightly. The gasket can be removed from the upper bowl by slipping a small screwdriver under the edge of the gasket and prying it off as shown in Fig. 5. A replacement can be obtained from your local service center and installed by simply pushing the gasket on.

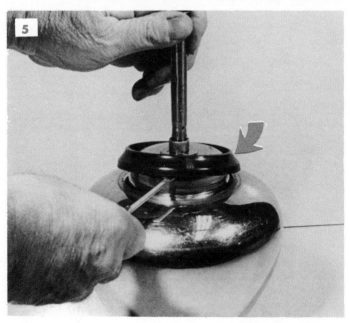

Step 2. If water is not rising due to misadjusted low-heat control, turn the coffee maker upside down and locate the "low-heat" adjustment screw, (Fig. 4). Loosen the locking nut with your long-nose pliers and turn the screw counterclockwise a couple of turns. Test the coffee maker as before, starting with cool water. Water should all rise to upper bowl, switch should snap to low, and water return to lower bowl. If coffee maker does not cycle in this manner, readjust low-heat adjusting screw as above and retest. When coffee maker cycles properly, the water in the bowl should be at a temperature of between 165 and 180 degrees. Test with your thermometer and adjust the low-heat adjustment screw until the water is maintained between these two temperatures. Adjustment screw must be turned clockwise to decrease temperature and counterclockwise to increase. When proper adjustment is found, tighten the locking nut on the adjustment screw being careful not to change the position of the screw itself.

Water Rises But Unit Does Not Switch to Low

This symptom is caused by misadjustment of the high-heat adjusting screw.

Step 1. Loosen locking nut on high-heat adjusting screw and turn screw clockwise a turn at a time, retesting after each turn, until the high-low switch functions properly. Then retighten the locking nut without moving the adjusting screw.

Water Rises But Coffee Does not Return to Lower Bowl

If the water rises satisfactorily but the coffee does not return to the lower bowl or is extremely slow in returning, the gasket is bad.

Step 1. Remove gasket as shown in Fig. 5 and replace with a new gasket.

Coffee Maker Does Not Heat At All

If coffee maker does not heat at all, the trouble can be: misadjusted high- and low-heat adjustment screws, loose connections inside the base, a bad cord, or a burned out heating element.

Step 1. Test the cord for continuity as described in Section 1 and shown in Fig. 6. Replace with a new cord or replace plugs as indicated.

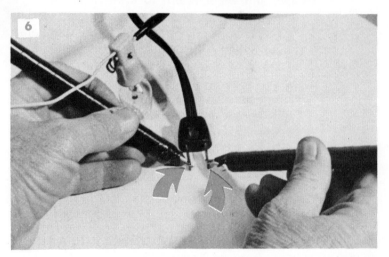

Step 2. If cord is tested and seems OK, remove the bottom plate of the base as shown in Fig. 7.

Step 3. Plug in the continuity tester and apply the probe tips to the two terminals of the heating element as shown in Fig. 8. A continuity indication here (test lamp lit) indicates that the heating element is good; no light indicates an open heating element and the unit will have to be further disassembled to replace the heating element.

Step 4. If the heating element tests good in Step 3, plug in the coffee maker line cord and connect to an outlet. Using the voltage probes, test the circuit for voltage at the same two terminals as before (Fig. 8). No voltage at these points indicates that the switching mechanism is faulty or the contact points are not closing or are dirty. Unplug the cord from the socket and inspect the points to see if they are closing. They should be closed at both the high- and low-heat settings of the "High-Low" switch. If the contacts are closed, clean them with a piece of fine sandpaper and finish polishing them with a strip of cardboard as shown in Fig. 9. Retest for voltage at heater terminals as before. If there is still no voltage at the heater terminals the connections inside the base must be checked.

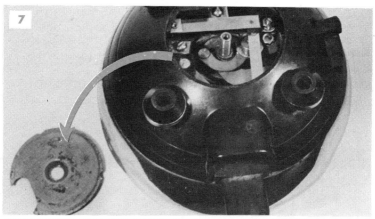

Step 5. Remove the two screws at the heating element terminals. Lift the bakelite base assembly at the side opposite the "High-Low" switch and slide it forward as shown in Fig. 10. Check the internal connections shown in Fig. 11 for tightness.

If, in Step 3, the heating element test indicated an open heating element, an exact replacement heating element will have to be obtained from the manufacturer's service center. To remove the faulty element proceed as follows:

Remove the nut on the center post shown in Fig. 12, and the nut holding the switch assembly. Lift off switch assem-

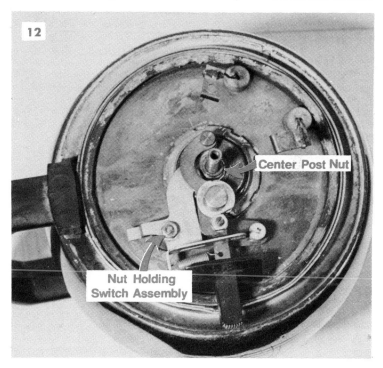

bly as shown in Fig. 13. Unscrew the retaining rings shown in Fig. 13, unscrew the stud holding the thermostat blade and lift out the heating element as shown in Fig. 14. Place the replacement element carefully in position and replace the retaining rings. Reassembly is the opposite of disassembly and is obvious from this point. Make sure that all nuts and screws are properly tightened. When reassembly is complete, fill the lower bowl with water and retest for proper heat adjustments as described previously.

Element Cover
Retaining Rings

PERCOLATORS

Percolators, although varying in size, shape, and capacity, all have essentially the same electrical system (Fig. 15). The electrical system is shown in Fig. 16. While the coffee maker is cold, the thermostat contacts remain closed shorting the "keeps hot" element out of the circuit. Therefore, the full supply voltage is supplied to the pump heater and percolation starts. When the proper temperature to open the thermostat (selected brew strength) is reached, the bending blade of the thermostat forces the contact points open

14

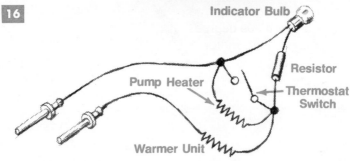

Indicator Bulb

Resistor

Pump Heater

Thermostat
Switch

Warmer Unit

and the voltage is applied to the "keeps hot" element in series
with the pump element. The total wattage is thus reduced to
maintain the coffee at serving temperature.

The usual complaints with this type coffee maker are:

1. Coffee tastes bitter,
2. Weak coffee,
3. Coffee boils or repercolates,
4. Will not operate at all,
5. Leaks.

Coffee Bitter

Bitter coffee is usually caused by the interior of the pot and pump unit being stained with residue from coffee. Inspect the basket and pump insert, and the interior for stains and residue and clean with a cleaner made especially for coffee pots. This cleaner is available at your local supermarket.

Weak Coffee

Weak coffee is caused by coffee grounds and residue in the heater well; starting the coffee with hot water instead of cool, or misadjusted cutoff temperature control. To adjust cutoff temperature, the following steps should be performed.

Step 1. Fill the pot with cool water. Put the lid on after removing the glass indicator in the lid. Hang your thermometer through the hole in the top of the lid so the tip of the thermometer is about 1 inch above the bottom of the pot. Put selector switch in "Strong" position and plug in the line cord. Temperature should rise to between 180 and 200 degrees.

Step 2. If test indicates that temperature should be changed, pry out the plug button in the base. Insert a small screwdriver through the hole in base and engage the slot in the temperature-control adjusting screw (Fig. 17). Turning the screw clockwise lowers the temperature and turning counterclockwise raises the temperature. One quarter turn of the screw changes the temperature about 20 degrees. Now reflll the pot with cool tap water and retest with the thermometer.

Coffee Repercolates

Step 3. Check for proper cutoff temperature as in Step 2.

Step 4. Remove the base of the coffee maker by removing center screw on the bottom and lifting the

base straight off the unit. Place a small piece of cardboard between the contacts of the thermostat to hold them open. Use the continuity tester and place one probe on each end of the end connections of the "keeps hot" heating element as shown in Fig. 18. An open indication (no light) shows that the "keeps hot" element is defective and must be replaced. Remove the element and install an exact replacement. The element must be placed flush and tight against the bottom of the pot under the metal guides exactly like the old element.

Step 5. Reassemble the base to the pot. When repositioning the base assembly, set the temperature-control arm so the slot points directly at the center of the pot, set the flavor selector lever at "Medium" and gently lower the base so that the pin on the selector lever engages in the slot. Now retest the percolator as in Step 2 for proper temperature regulation.

Will Not Operate

Step 6. Check the cord set for continuity. Remove bottom as described in Step 4. Check internal cord terminals for burned or corroded connections. Clean and retighten if corroded or burned or replace with new terminal block.

Step 7. Place probes of continuity tester on the two terminals of the pump heating unit as shown in Fig. 19. If pump heating element shows "no continuity", the element is bad. This element in late model coffee makers, is brazed into the bottom of the pot. In this type, no repairs are possible and the entire coffee maker must be discarded. On older models, the pump unit can be replaced.

18

Temperature-Control Arm

Cardboard Between Contacts

Metal Guides for Element

"Keeps-Hot" Element

Step 8. If replacement is possible, remove the two wires leading from the pump element to the thermostat and to the plug terminal at the thermostat and terminal.

Step 9. Remove the large hexagonal nut on the top of the pump assembly. You will find this nut inside the coffee pot at the bottom. Turn the pot upside down again and lift out the pump heater. The replacement is reinstalled in the reverse manner. The element is put in place, the inside nut tightened, and the connecting leads placed back on the plug and thermostat terminal screws.

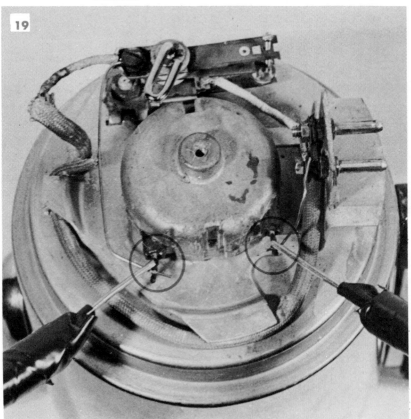

Coffee Maker Leaks

Leaks in the coffee maker are most likely to occur around the glass-tubing level gauge on the side of the pot under the handle.

Step 10. Remove the bakelite cover over the gauge tube by removing the top screw and the bottom slotted nut that holds the handle. The slotted round nut at the bottom can be quite a problem if you do not have the special tool necessary to remove it. The entire handle can now be pulled out and the gauge tube removed and inspected. The rubber grommet, into which the glass tube fits, may have to be replaced. Any leaks in the pot itself cannot be repaired unless you are prepared to weld stainless steel.

SECTION

Electric Griddles

The electric griddle (Fig. 1) resembles the electric skillet in construction and operation. The griddle consists of a cast aluminum base with a sealed heating element. The griddle is usually covered with *Teflon* to help prevent food sticking to the cooking surface. A removable grease catcher pan is located under a hole in the griddle through which excess grease is drained from the griddle during cooking. The grease catcher is shown removed in Fig. 2. The temperature-control thermostat is contained in a probe plug shown with the cover removed in Fig. 3.

The usual complaints with the electric griddle are:
1. Heat too high,
2. Heat too low,
3. No heat.

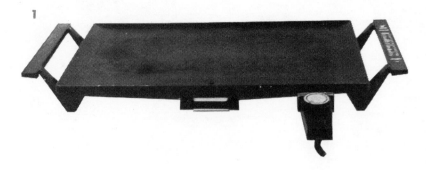

1

HEAT TOO HIGH

Heat too high is caused by a defective or misadjusted thermostat. There is no adjustment than can be easily made to the thermostat in the probe plug. The thermostat in this type of probe plug is actuated by a copper rod that extends into the aluminum probe itself, which pushes on a small vertical tab attached to the control's movable contact spring. The only adjustment to this type of thermostat is bending the tab on the contact spring blade to change the position of the blade.

Step 1. Remove the four screws holding the cover of the probe assembly and remove the cover (Fig. 4).

Step 2. Examine the thermostat assembly (Fig. 5) and locate the copper rod extending from the heat-probe to the small tab which is attached at a right angle to the contact spring.

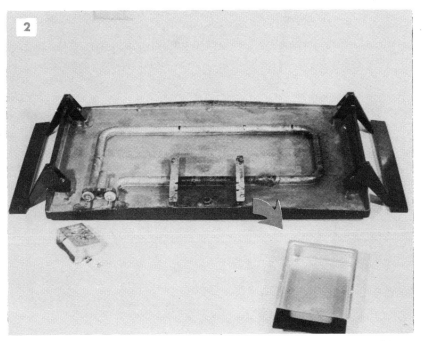

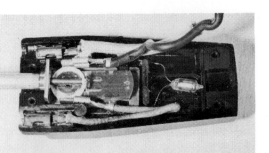

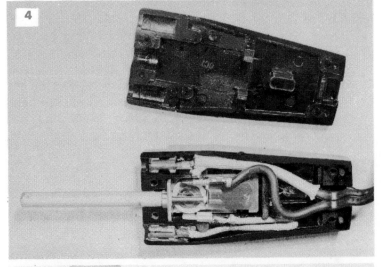

Step 3. Having located the adjustment tab in Step 2, grasp the tab with the tips of your long-nose pliers. Hold the contact spring down with your finger and carefully bend the tab *away from the heat probe.* A small amount of bending changes the temperature several degrees so don't bend the tab too much.

Step 4. Put the cover back on the plug assembly and test the griddle. This is pretty much a guesswork test to check the temperature of the griddle. There is no way to test the temperature of the griddle without an elaborate thermocouple testing setup, which only factory servicemen have available. The best test is to have the family cook judge whether the temperature is right as he or she cooks. If the temperature is still too high, repeat Steps 3 and 4 until the temperature is satisfactory.

HEAT TOO LOW

The reasons for the heat of the griddle being too low may be the opposite as for "Heat Too High," but, in addition too low heat may be caused by a defective cord, burned or corroded plug contacts, or a defective wall socket.

Step 1. Examine the cord carefully looking for cracks in the insulation. If the insulation is cracked or broken, the strands of wire inside the insulation may be partially broken, in which case the cord cannot pass enough current to properly heat the heating element.

Step 2. If the cord appears to be OK, remove the cover of the probe plug as instructed in Step 1 under "Heat Too High" procedure. Examine the internal connections of the cord for partially broken wires, burned contacts, or loose push-on connectors. If any of the conditions of Step 1 or Step 2 exist, the cord must be replaced. An exact replacement cord will contain the solderless push-on connectors attached and only requires pushing the connectors on to the terminals in the plug assembly. Replacement heater cords can be obtained at most hardware stores and at electrical appliance stores.

Step 3. If the cord is not the problem, the "Heat Too Low" symptom is caused by an improperly adjusted thermostat. The adjustment is made in the same manner as the adjustment for "Heat Too High" previously described. The only difference is that the small vertical tab (Fig. 5) on the thermostat blade must be bent slightly *toward the probe*—the opposite of the "Heat Too High" adjustment.

Step 4. Replace the cover on the probe plug and test the griddle under cooking conditions as previously described. Several repetitions of the bending procedures may be required before you get it right.

NO HEAT

Not heat at all may be caused by:
1. Defective wall socket or a blown fuse in the house circuit.
2. A defective cord or plug or broken or loose connections in the probe plug or cord plug.
3. Open, or burned out, heating element in the griddle.

In cases where the symptom is "No Heat," the heating element should be checked first. If the heating element is defective, there is no repair that can be made since the element is cast into the base and completely sealed.

Step 1. Turn the griddle upside down and remove the two screws holding the guard over the heating element prongs. Plug in your continuity tester. *Caution: Do not touch the tips of the continuity probes. Handle only by the taped handles.* Test the continuity tester by touching the tips of the probes together. The lamp should light if the tester is working. Touch the tips of the probes

to the two heater prongs (one probe tip on each prong) of the griddle (Fig. 6). A continuity reading at these points (lamp in tester lit) means that the heating element is OK. A reading of no continuity (lamp in tester not lit) means that the heating element is open and there are no repairs that can be made.

Step 2. Test the wall receptacle that you will use as shown in Fig. 7 with your voltage tester. The tester should light if the wall receptacle is serviceable or the house fuse is not blown. Now plug in the cord of the griddle in the wall receptacle but do not insert the probe plug into the griddle. Turn the thermostat control knob to an

"ON" position. Insert the tips of the voltage tester into the sockets of the probe plug as shown in Fig. 8. If the tester lamp lights, the cord and plug are OK. If there is no light, either the cord or the probe-plug assembly is defective and the job requires further testing.

Step 3. Unplug the cord from the wall receptacle. Remove the cover from the probe plug as shown previously in Fig. 4. Locate the terminals where the cord is connected inside the plug. Check the wires for broken or burned connections. If any connections are found loose or broken, replace the cord with an exact replacement cord. The cord is connected by push-on terminals which come already on the ends of the cord.

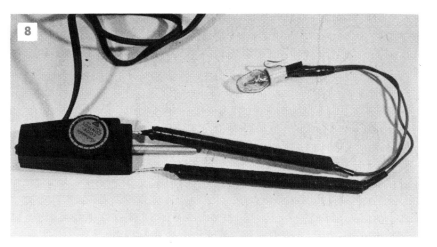

Step 4. If the cord is apparently good, following the foregoing examination or replacement, plug the cord into the wall receptacle and touch the cord terminations inside the probe plug with the tips of the voltage tester probe (Fig. 9). If the cord is good, the tester lamp will light. If there is no indication, the cord is bad requiring cord replacement as described in Step 3.

Step 5. If the test in Step 4 shows voltage at the cord terminals and there is no voltage at the probe plug sockets as shown in Fig. 8, the thermostat is open. Check to be sure the contacts on the thermostat are closed. If not, bend the adjustment tab as described previously until they close. If they are closed but no voltage is detected at the plug sockets, clean the contacts with fine sandpaper and polish with a cardboard strip as instructed in Section 1 of this book. The thermostat will have to be readjusted as previously instructed in this Section to cut off at the proper temperature. If you still cannot get voltage through the contacts after cleaning and adjustment, the entire probe-plug assembly will have to be replaced.

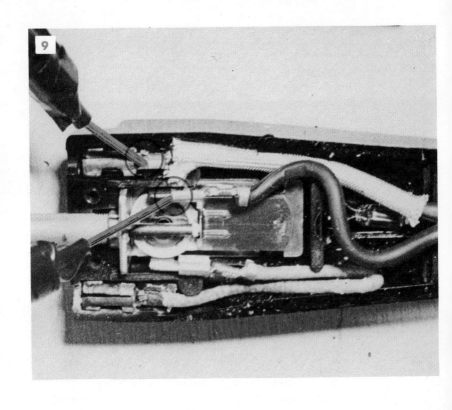